Also available by Katie Price,

and published by Random House Children's Books:

Katie Price's Perfect Ponies series:

1. Here Comes the Bride

2. Little Treasures

3. Fancy Dress Ponies

4. Pony Club Weekend

KATIE PRICE'S PERFECT PONIES: MY PONY CARE BOOK
A RED FOX BOOK 978 1 862 30365 2

Published in Great Britain by Red Fox,
an imprint of Random House Children's Books
A Random House Group Company

This edition published 2007

1 3 5 7 9 10 8 6 4 2

Red Fox Books are published by Random House Children's Books,
61–63 Uxbridge Road, London W5 5SA

www.**kids**at**randomhouse**.co.uk
www.katiesperfectponies.co.uk
www.rbooks.co.uk

Addresses for companies within The Random House Group Limited can be found at: www.randomhouse.co.uk/offices.htm

THE RANDOM HOUSE GROUP Limited Reg. No. 954009

A CIP catalogue record for this book is available from the British Library.

Printed and bound in Singapore

This book is a general guide to pony care and is not a substitute for nor should it be relied on as professional advice. Always consult a qualified professional riding instructor. We would also advise that you wear a protective riding hat whenever you are handling any pony. The author and publishers disclaim, as far as the law allows, any liability arising directly or indirectly from the use or misuse of the information contained in this book.

Katie Price's
Perfect Ponies

My Pony Care Book

RED FOX

Hi!

My name is Katie and I love ponies! I met my first ponies when I was seven years old and I went to a riding stables for the first time ever. From that minute onwards, I was totally horse-mad. I had pictures of horses on almost everything I owned: pencil cases, pens, bags, notebooks . . . you name it, I had a pony picture on it! My bedroom walls were plastered with pictures of horses, and I longed for a pony of my own to love.

I was really lucky; my mum let me have a pony on loan when I was eleven. Now I'm grown up – I'm a mum myself – but I still have horses. And I still want to surround them with lots and lots of love.

Over the years I've learned an awful lot. I learned how to ride, of course. But I've also found out how to look after ponies and horses: how to groom them, feed them, exercise them, and take care of them when they're not well. Now I want to share what I know with you so that if you are lucky enough to have a pony in your life, your pony will also be lucky enough to have you in his life!

Love,

Katie xxx

Me and my horses

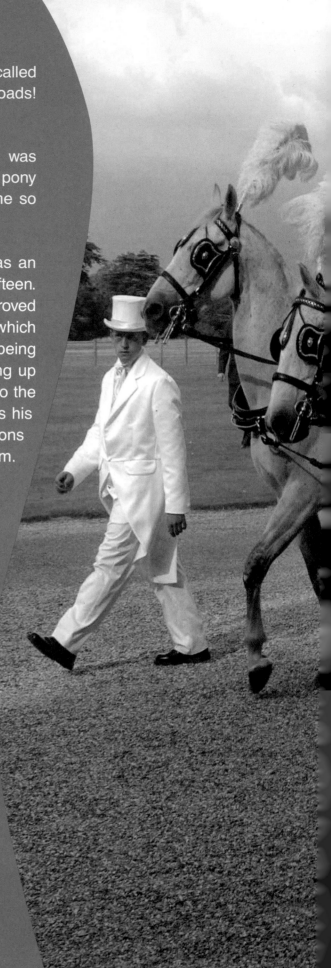

The first pony I ever rode was at the riding school and he was called Oscar. He used to bomb off with me and I fell off him loads! But that's how everyone learns to ride.

Star was the first pony I had to look after every day. He was eighteen years old and the scruffiest, shabbiest, most lovable pony ever. I wanted to be with him all day every day. He taught me so much and I will never, ever forget him.

The first horse I actually owned was also called Star! He was an ex-racehorse and Mum agreed to buy him for me when I was fifteen. I'd had ponies and horses on loan for over four years so I had proved I was serious about it and really did look after them properly, which is ever so important. No one should buy a horse without being prepared to do all the work that is necessary. It means getting up early – even on cold, wet winter mornings – and going down to the field or stables and making sure your pony is all right and has his breakfast. I loved Star lots, but he had problems with the tendons in his legs, so I spent more time looking after him than riding him.

It's not all work, though. Riding is such fun! I love going for long rides. Just me and my horse, galloping across the fields. Perfect!

Star was an ex-racehorse!

I love horses and ponies so much I even had horses at my wedding. I arrived at the ceremony in a Cinderella carriage pulled by beautiful grey horses. Look!

Me and my horses

Now I've got six horses and ponies: four horses and two ponies.
One – a gorgeous, furry Shetland called Rosie – is for my son, Harvey.

My newest horse is Duke. He's a 17-1 black gelding.
Here are the other horses in my life:

Jelly – she's a
16-2 chestnut mare

Pepsi is an ex-polo
pony. She's a 14-2
dark bay mare

Sally – she's a
16-2 black mare

Tyke – he's an
18 bay gelding

So, you see, I've got lots of ponies and horses in my life, and I am so proud of all of them. But I've also had to work very hard to look after them properly, and now it's time to pass some of my tips on to you. I hope you too, will have lives filled with horses and ponies.

By the way, all through this book, I've called ponies 'he' and 'him', but obviously everything applies to your favourite mares too. I've got both mares and geldings myself.

Rosie

Do you own your own pony?

If you do, you are very lucky indeed. But you will also know that loving your pony isn't enough on its own - you also have to know how to look after him. Do make sure you learn all about how to care for your special friend.

Read pony magazines.

Ask at your riding school about stable management lessons.

Join your local Pony Club.

Take riding lessons.

Don't feel shy about asking experienced owners for help.

Read this book! And my pony story books.

But you don't have to own your own pony to be pony-mad. Here are some other ways to spend time with ponies.

Riding holidays

Be totally pony-mad for a week! It's fabulous to live, breathe and sleep ponies day after day in a special holiday centre.

Riding schools

This is how I began, with lessons and rides. You can also ask if you can help with the ponies by mucking out stables or tacking up.

Own your own pony days

Lots of riding schools have special days in the holidays when you can 'own' your favourite pony. You get to fetch him in from the field, groom him, tack him up – and ride him.

Ponies on loan

This is how I got my first pony, Star. It's like having your own pony because you are totally responsible for looking after him every day, but the pony still belongs to the original owner.

'Share' a pony

Some owners also look for *sharers*, so you agree to look after the pony for two or three days each week and they look after him on the other days.

Pony-mad with no ponies around?

Don't give up! You can still read books and magazines and learn lots about ponies and horses. Why don't you cut out or copy your favourite pictures and stick them in an album? Get together with your mates, too, to talk ponies, ponies, ponies!

All about ponies

The best pony for you is always a pony you love. But it's also important that you ride a pony that is right for you. Some riders want a steady, safe ride, especially if they are just beginning. Other riders want a challenge, or to race about and jump.

Most people learn to ride at a riding school and most riding schools in Britain have lots of ponies who live out in fields in our weather quite happily and are 'good doers' – ponies that don't cost you a fortune in bedding, feed and rugs!

My first pony, Star, was a New Forest pony. Other types of British pony you might meet are Welsh ponies, Dales or Fells ponies, Highland ponies, Exmoors, Dartmoors or Connemaras. Or the pony you ride might be a mix of these breeds. And every stable has a few Shetland ponies – the breed that everyone knows and loves. My son's pony, Rosie, is a Shetland. Woolly, mischievous and very very huggable, they are the smallest native-bred ponies. Watch out though – they are great escape artists. If there's a hole in the hedge, they'll find it!

Exmoor

So huggable!

KATIE'S TIP

If you buy or loan a pony, you and your pony pal will want to have lots of fun together so make sure you find a pony that is perfect for you. Can you ride well enough for a competition pony? Or would you be better with a safe schoolmaster? There's no point buying a posh pony you can't ride.

Shetland

Welsh

9

Parts of a horse

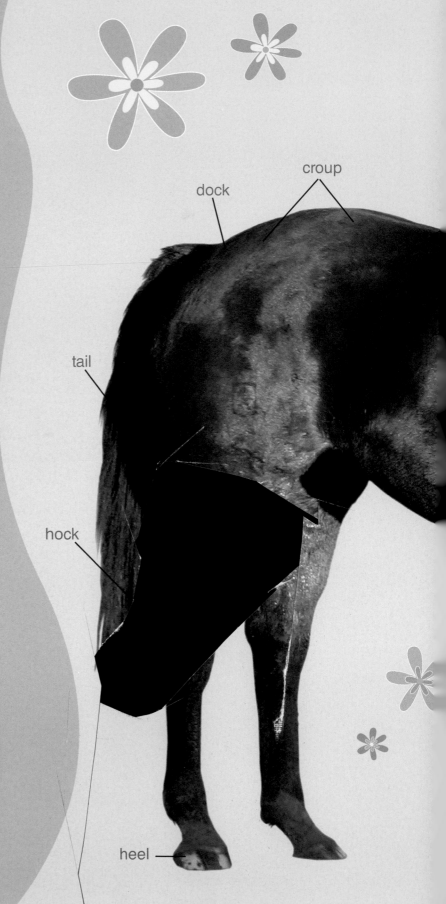

dock

croup

tail

hock

heel

KATIE'S TIP

Every pony-lover should know the main parts of a horse. If your pony has an injury, for example, you need to be able to tell the vet where he has hurt himself.

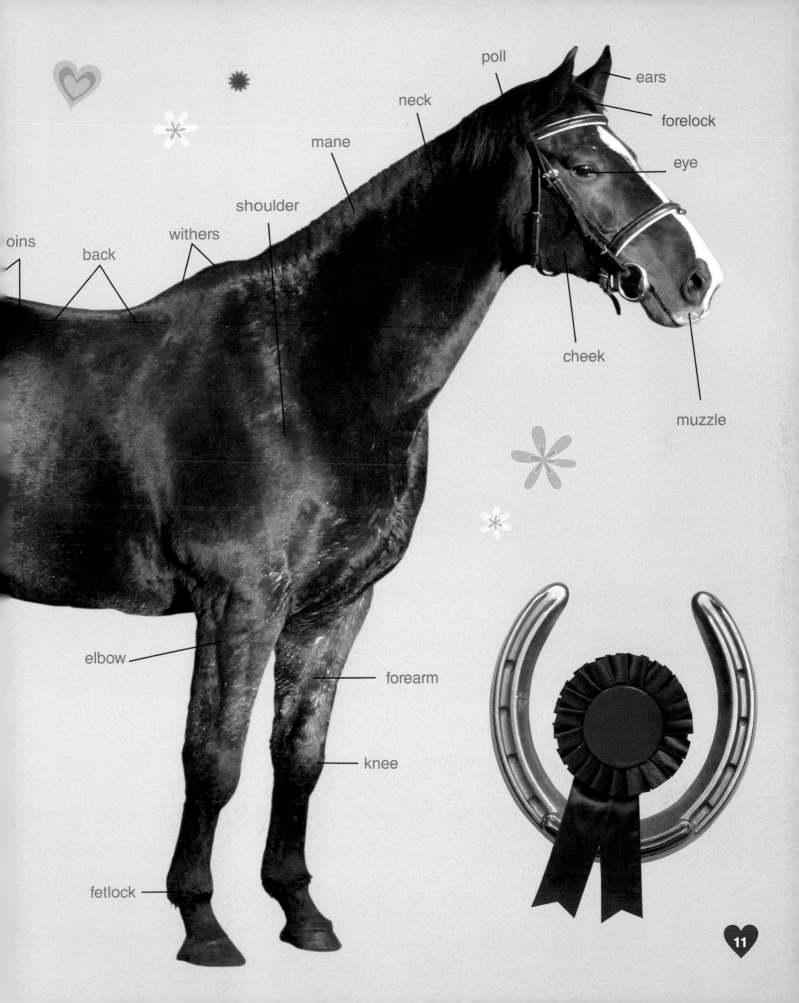

poll

neck

ears

forelock

mane

eye

shoulder

withers

oins

back

cheek

muzzle

elbow

forearm

knee

fetlock

11

Other horsey terms

To describe your favourite pony to someone else, you need to know some of the terms used. These details will also be on your pony's passport.

Colours

Black – like my horses Duke, Sally and Rosie.

Bay – never call a brown horse 'brown'.

Chestnut – glossy red, like my horse Jelly.

Grey – all white horses are called greys.

Dun – mouse-coloured with a black mane and tail.

Palomino - golden-coloured.

Roan – a speckly mix of chestnut or bay with black or white hairs.

piebald – like a magpie! Black and white patches.

skewbald – like piebalds but with brown or chestnut patches.

Sizes

Except for Shetland ponies, who are measured in inches, the height of a pony or horse is always given in 'hands'. One hand equals four inches, or ten centimetres, and your pony's height is the distance between the ground and the highest point of his withers. So a pony could be described as being '12 hands', or a horse as '16-2' which would mean 16 hands plus 2 inches. You can use a special measuring stick to find out your favourite pony's exact height. My biggest horse at the moment is Tyke; he's a whopping 18 hands!

Measure here - at the withers.

Markings

Common markings include

A blaze: a white mark right down the face, as above.

A star: a white mark on the forehead.

A snip: a little white mark right between your pony's nostrils.

Look at this cute foal!

KATIE'S TIP

If you buy a young pony, you should not try and ride him until he is about four years old. A young horse is usually backed (taught to wear a saddle and have a rider on its back) when they are three years old, but not ridden for another year. Until you can ride your pony, you can still spend lots of time with him and build up a real bond between the two of you.

Ages

- a foal is any horse or pony up to one year old

- a colt is a young boy pony up to the age of three

- a filly is a young girl pony up to the age of three

- when colts are neutered so they can't breed with mares, they are called geldings

- a male horse with all his bits is a stallion

- a female horse aged over three is a mare

What your pony needs

All ponies need the same basic things:

A home with shelter from the bad weather and sun. This can be a stable or a field, but remember that ponies like to be outdoors so even stabled ponies will want to go out every day.

Feed Make sure your pony always has the right amount to eat. This will vary according to the type of pony he is, the time of year and what you want him to do.

Water Ponies should always be able to get a drink of water whenever they want.

Daily care Yes, I do mean *daily*. There's no point having a pony of your own if you can't come and see him every day.

Health care This means looking after his vaccinations, making sure his feet are in good condition and talking to your vet about anything else he needs. This is especially important if your pony is feeling poorly.

Exercise Riding is fun for you, but it's also good exercise for your pony. Ponies that don't do any work can get very fat and lazy.

And . . .

. . . don't forget to give your pony **LOTS OF HUGS AND KISSES**. Ponies love to have special friends who they see regularly. If your favourite pony is at a riding school and you only see him once a week, make sure he knows how much you love him when you do see him.

Safety First

Ponies are big animals and you should always remember that they can hurt you. They won't mean to, but it's better to be safe than sorry.

● *Wear strong shoes or boots*
It's no fun if a pony steps on your toes – *ouch!* Leave your best shoes at home and wear the right kind of boots down at the stables.

●*Don't walk round the back of a pony without him knowing you are there*
A pony can kick out if you frighten him. Ponies can't see right behind them, so for all they know, you might be a dangerous animal creeping up on them! If in doubt, a pony will kick out and run away. To walk past safely, make sure the pony knows you are there, touch him on the haunches and speak softly to him. Ask him to step to the side and then move past slowly.

●*Wear boots with a small heel for riding in*
This is really important. If you ride in the wrong kind of boots, you could get your foot stuck in the stirrup, which would be dangerous if your pony slips and you fall off. You can buy long riding boots or short jodhpur boots.

● *Always wear an approved riding helmet*
Whenever you are dealing with ponies you should always wear a protective hat. And never ride without wearing a proper riding helmet. If you fall off (everyone does sometimes), this will protect your head. It's very very important. Nowadays you can buy really funky silk covers for your riding helmet, so that you look cool and fashionable. And you can even add your own special touches to the covers.

Do ask your parent or other responsible adult to help you do this.

How to make your riding hat look really cool and special

1. Sew or stick on lots and lots of sparkly sequins so that your hat looks really fabulous and glittery.

2. Sew on lots of little imitation pearls or beads to spell out your name, your initial or your pony's name.

3. Use embroidery and silky thread to sew your name or your pony's name on a plain silk. If you use alternating colours, this can look really lovely.

Daily care

Catching your pony

Your pony will learn to look out for you if you always come at the same time every day. Stand at the gate and call his name, and he should come over to you. But ponies also like being with their mates or just eating grass – so you will probably have to go over to him sometimes to catch him.

- Walk over slowly; don't run or scream or you might frighten him.

- Approach from the head end at a slight angle so he can easily see you.

- Talk to him, and give him a pat before you try to put on the headcollar.

- Stand at his left-hand side, and slip the lead rein over his neck first.

- Put on the headcollar and do it up properly, with the end of the strap tucked in.

- Hug your pony for being so good!

KATIE'S TIP

If your pony is a problem to catch, never tell him off when you do finally catch him or he'll think that being caught means being told off.

Leading your pony

All ponies should learn how to lead – and so should you. If you aren't sure you can control your pony, always take someone more experienced with you when you go to catch him.

A pony can be frightened by the silliest things! On a windy day, a pile of leaves blowing up can be enough to make him want to run away. Or another pony could startle him.

Here's how to lead a pony properly:

- Always wear a riding hat and gloves when leading a pony.

- Lead from his left-hand side.

- Walk level with his shoulder. If you walk in front, and he gets frightened and rushes forward, he could bash into you and knock you over. If you walk too far behind, he could race off without you.

Wrong way to lead

- Hold the lead rein with your right hand near the headcollar. Hold the other end off the ground with your left hand.

- Don't ever let the loose end trail down round your pony's legs or he could get tangled up in it.

- Make sure your hand is facing downwards over the lead rein. This gives the best control if your pony throws his head up in the air.

- Never, ever wrap the lead rein around your wrist or hand. You could lose your fingers if your pony suddenly bombs off!

- Only lead one pony at a time. It might look clever to lead two at once, but no one can properly control more than one pony at a time.

Right way to lead

19

Tying up your pony

When you bring your pony in from the field, or out from his stable, you will need to tie him up to groom him and to tack him up.

- *DO* use a quick-release knot to tie him up. These are easy to undo in a hurry.

- *DON'T* ever tie him to a gate or door that he could pull open.

- *DO* always tie a loop of baling twine to the ring or fence first and then tie him to this. This means he can break free in an emergency.

- *DON'T* tie him up to a fence where other ponies can come and talk to him from the other side. He could get excited and put his foot through the fence.

- *DON'T* leave your pony for long periods on his own while he is tied up.

How to tie a quick-release knot.

1. Put the lead rein through the loop of twine and make a loop out of the loose end.

2. Take the end underneath the rope and make another loop.

3. Now push this loop through the first loop.

4. To untie this in a hurry, just pull the loose end.

KATIE'S TIP

Feed the loose end through the loop if your pony likes to untie the knot with his teeth. You don't want him to escape!

Grooming your pony

Make your pony feel really pampered! Ponies love being groomed and it is also very good for their skin so it helps them to stay healthy. If you are going to put a saddle or a rug on, it is very important to get rid of all the mucky bits of mud that might make this uncomfy for him.

Your pony's grooming kit

Your pony should have his own set of brushes and grooming tools. If you have your own pony, you can keep all your gear together in a big box and make it really special. Why not get a big picture of your favourite pony and stick it on the box to let everyone know that these are his things?

- Paint his name on the box with poster paint. And add little horseshoes or your own painting of your pony. Let your imagination run wild!

- Decorate your locker with your favourite pictures of you and your pony in action. Or use pictures of gorgeous ponies that you have cut out from magazines.

- Pin up the rosettes you win on your locker so you can feel extra-proud of your pony every time you go and get his brushes.

Ask an adult to help you cut horseshoe shapes out of cooking foil.

Grooming your pony

This is how I like to groom my horses and ponies. I love making them look really pretty!

Use a **hoofpick** to pick mud or stones out of your pony's feet. Never forget to do this, it's really important. Begin at the heel and use the hoofpick towards the toe. Avoid jabbing your pony in the frog.

KATIE'S TIP

When picking out a pony's feet, always do them in the same order and your pony will soon begin to pick his feet up for you in the right order. Ponies are so clever!

Royston
FUNNELL RANGE

● Use the **currycomb** to remove all the dried mud, dirt and loose hair that is on his coat – but don't use this on your pony's face or soft bits of his body as it could hurt him. Start on the neck and work towards the back. Don't ever use a plastic currycomb on a clipped pony.

● Now brush him all over with the **dandy brush**. That's the stiff brush, so again not to be used on a clipped pony. Don't be afraid to put some welly into it – if you watch ponies grooming each other, they use their teeth! But make sure you are very careful around any tender bits.

● Now use the softer **body brush**. The hairs on this brush go right through to your pony's skin and bring up the oils in his coat to make him look shiny. Don't use this in the winter if your pony is living in a field, because he needs these oils then to help keep him warm and waterproof. Use this brush in short strokes that follow the lay of your pony's coat.

● Brush out the mane and tail with the body brush. Hold the tail out to one side and brush just a few strands at a time.

● Comb through your pony's mane with a **mane comb**.

● Clean round your pony's eyes with a **damp sponge** or pad. Then use another sponge for his bottom.

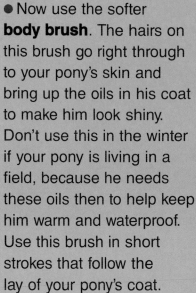

Bathing your pony

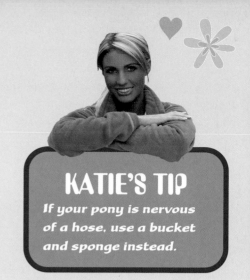

KATIE'S TIP
If your pony is nervous of a hose, use a bucket and sponge instead.

For shows or special events, you might want to give your pony a bath before you set out. This can be a lot of fun too.

• **DON'T** ever bath a pony in the winter if he has to live out. You could wash the oils out of his coat – oils that he needs to keep warm and cosy.

• **DO** use a hose with a steady stream of water that isn't too fierce. You don't want to frighten your pony.

• **DO** start by wetting his hooves and gradually move the hose up higher.

• **DON'T** get the lather too near your pony's eyes as you rub special horse shampoo all over him with wet sponges and body brushes.

• **DO** rinse off thoroughly. Use a sweat scraper to remove excess water, and towel-dry his legs and belly.

• **DON'T** let your pony stand around all wet once you have finished. Walk or run him up and down to help him dry. He will probably stand and shake himself like a dog too, so watch out!

Washing a pony's tail

Washing a pony's tail can be a very wet, messy business if your pony won't stand still! Begin by wetting as much of the tail as possible in a bucket of water, but you will still need a sponge to wet down the top. The shampoo must be washed out properly and you will probably need to dunk his tail in several buckets of water to get it all out.

For special occasions

When I go to a big party, I really like to look my best – and I like my ponies and horses to look extra-fantastic too sometimes.

Plaiting

Plaiting your pony's mane and tail can look really cool.
First tie up your pony using a quick-release knot and brush out any tangles in his mane.

How to plait his mane

1. Dampen the mane and divide it into sections. Put little rubber plaiting bands round each section.

2. Now plait each section, just like you would plait your own hair or your friend's. Fasten the end with a small rubber band.

3. Lastly, fold the plait back on itself to form a small ball and wrap a band around it to keep it in place.

1. 2. 3.

Decorate the plaits

Use ribbon to tie a bow onto each plait.
Or weave a ribbon into each plait before you roll it up.

Plaiting a tail

1. Brush out all the tangles, then take a section of hair from the centre at the very top and plait with a few strands from each side. Each time you make a plait, take a few more strands from the side.

2. The top part of your pony's tail is made of bone. When you are about two-thirds of the way down this part, just plait the centre hairs so that the finished plait hangs down over the rest of his tail.

3. Fasten the end of the plait, and fold the end underneath.

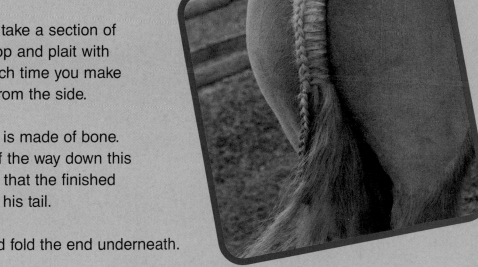

1.

2.

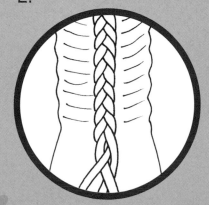

3.

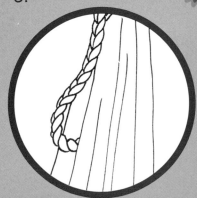

Your pony's headcollar

Ponies live in the wild with just their own coats for protection. But if we keep them in fields or stables and like to ride them, they will need lots of tack and other gear.

Every pony needs a headcollar and a lead rein so you can catch him, lead him and tie him up safely. You can buy headcollars in all sorts of colours nowadays. I like to match the colour of each headcollar with the same colour lead rein.

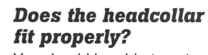

Does the headcollar fit properly?

You should be able to put two fingers between the noseband and your pony's nose and two fingers below the cheekbone. If you can't, it is too tight and will be uncomfy for your pony. If it's too loose, your pony might be able to pull his head through and get away from you when you are leading him.

Your pony's bridle

When you ride your pony, you will need to fit a bridle onto his head. This holds the bit in his mouth in the right place and your reins are attached to the bit rings to help you control your pony.

Make your pony smile
Does the bit fit properly? If it does, it should just make the corners of your pony's mouth crinkle up like he is smiling.

How to put a bridle on your pony

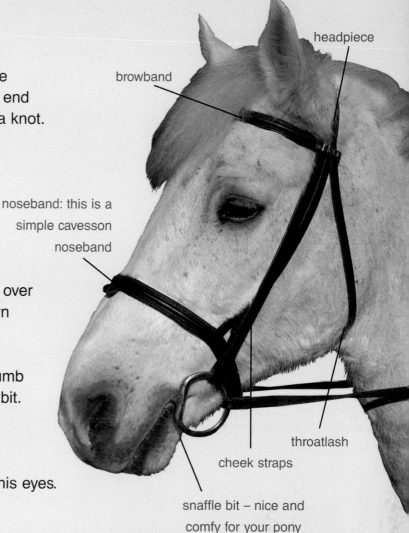

- headpiece
- browband
- noseband: this is a simple cavesson noseband
- throatlash
- cheek straps
- snaffle bit – nice and comfy for your pony

- Put the bridle on after the saddle.

- It's really important to untie the lead rein from the wall before you begin to tack up. Either hold the end or simply thread it through the loop but without a knot.

- Stand to the left-hand side and put the reins over your pony's head.

- Unbuckle the headcollar and loop it round your pony's neck while you fit the bridle.

- Hold your right hand under the pony's head and over his nose so you can hold the bridle halfway down with this hand. Hold the bit in your left hand.

- Gently open your pony's mouth with your left thumb in the corner of his mouth, then let him take the bit. Don't clunk it against his teeth!

- Use both hands to ease the bridle over his ears, making sure you don't let any straps bang onto his eyes.

- Pull his forelock through and over the browband.

- Do up the throatlash.

- Lastly, do up the noseband.

KATIE'S TIP

It is important to keep your pony's bridle really clean and supple. Clean it at least once a week, by taking it to pieces and cleaning each part separately. Don't put dirty tack on your pony.

Does the bridle fit properly?
You should be able to put:

- two fingers between the noseband and the top of your pony's nose

- two fingers between the noseband and your pony's cheekbones

- two fingers under the browband

- four fingers between the headpiece and your pony's cheek

Sparkly, special browbands

How to make your pony's browband look really special

● Wrap a silky ribbon round and round the browband for a very pretty look. I like to add a simple bow to this too. Pick your colour to match your pony. A bright pink (my favourite colour) looks fabulous on a dark bay, for instance. Or royal blue on a grey pony.

Do ask your parent or other responsible adult to help you do this.

● Cover your browband in black velvet and sew on little sequins for a fantastic, glittery effect. You could match this on your pony's noseband too. This looks really glamorous on a grey pony.

● Tie three small bows across the browband. This looks very pretty.

NB: be very careful to make sure that no rough edges are ever touching your pony's skin. You want him to look special but not to wear anything that could rub.

33

Your pony's saddle

Your pony will need his own saddle. It's really important that this fits properly or it could pinch him – or hurt his back. If in doubt, ask a saddler to check it out for you.

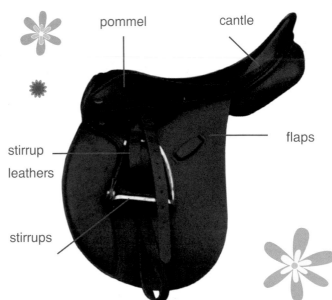

pommel

cantle

flaps

stirrup leathers

stirrups

KATIE'S TIP

Many ponies like to hold their breath and make themselves as fat as possible when you put a saddle on. So remember to check the girth is tight enough just before you get on. You'd feel really silly if the saddle slipped round when you put your foot in the stirrup!

How to put on a saddle

1. Make sure your pony's back is clean and mud-free.

2. Standing on his left side, place the saddle gently on his back, slightly forward of where it will sit, and then slide it back into position. Never pull it forward or it will rub your pony's coat the wrong way.

3. Let the girth hang down slowly on the far side – don't just chuck it over and let it bang down and hit your pony's legs. Walk round and check it isn't twisted or caught up in anything.

4. Carefully buckle up the girth on the left-hand side. Tighten it up more than once as no pony wants his girth pulled tight immediately.

Customized saddlecloths

Use a saddlecloth or numnah (a saddlecloth shaped like a saddle) underneath your saddle. I like to pick mine to match the colours of my horses. Tyke – who is a dark bay – looks fantastic in a bright red saddlecloth; while Jelly, who is a chestnut, looks fab in an emerald green one. I also like to customize them with my own special touches. Have fun and jazz up your pony's saddlecloth too!

Do ask your parent or other responsible adult to help you do this.

Make sure there are no rough stitches that could rub your pony's back.

- Use embroidery thread to sew your pony's name on his saddlecloth.
- Cut a pink feather boa into two and sew one half on the front edge of the saddlecloth and the other half on the back.
- Attach a funky fringe all round the edge – except for where the girth fits, of course.

Rugs

Don't let your pony feel cold in the winter! If your pony is clipped, you will have to give him a rug to keep him warm. A rug will also keep your pony dry and clean enough to tack up and ride. Ponies without rugs can get really, really muddy in fields!

An **outdoor rug** is completely waterproof. Make sure it fits properly, so your pony can roll in the field without the rug sliding to one side. Ponies look so sweet when they roll – with their feet all sticking up in the air!

If your pony lives in a stable, he will probably need a **stable rug** for warmth as he can't run around to keep warm. Lots of these are just like big, cosy duvets – I love to see my horses all tucked up and ready for the night!

How to put on a rug

It's important to know how to do this properly or your pony could get frightened, or try and run off when you only have it half on. If you want to put a rug on a pony in a field, always tie him up first or he could tank off with the rug hanging round his neck.

- Fold the rug in half and let your pony see it so he knows what's going to happen.

- Place it over his withers, unfold it and pull it gently back into position. Never move it forwards or you will make the hairs on his back stick up the wrong way.

- Do up the front straps first.

- Then fasten the belly straps, crossing them underneath your pony's belly.

- Lastly do up the straps round his hind legs. These have to be looped round each other so they don't rub on his thighs.

Decorate your show rug

At shows, I like my horses and ponies to look really fantastic, so I pick rugs in colours that really suit them. Then I decorate them so that everyone can see how smart my ponies are.

- Embroider your name and your pony's name on the rug.

- Cut out and sew little hearts around your pony's name so everyone can see how much you love him!

Travelling your pony

It's really fun to take your pony to shows. But if you travel him in a trailer or horsebox, he may need to wear a rug to protect him from knocks and also help keep him clean. If you've got up at the crack of dawn to polish up your pony for a show, you won't want him to get all mucky on the journey! When you reach the show, you can also use the rug to keep him warm between classes.

travelling boots

To protect your pony's feet and legs on the journey, fit **travelling boots**, which come up right above his knees and hocks. These come in funky colours which you can match to the rug. You can also put a **tail bandage** on his tail (never leave this on though for more than a few hours as it can cut the circulation to your pony's tail).

KATIE'S TIP

If your pony hasn't worn travelling boots before, don't leave it until the day of the big show to let him try wearing them. Some ponies can be very silly when they first wear these boots and wave their feet up in the air or walk really oddly.

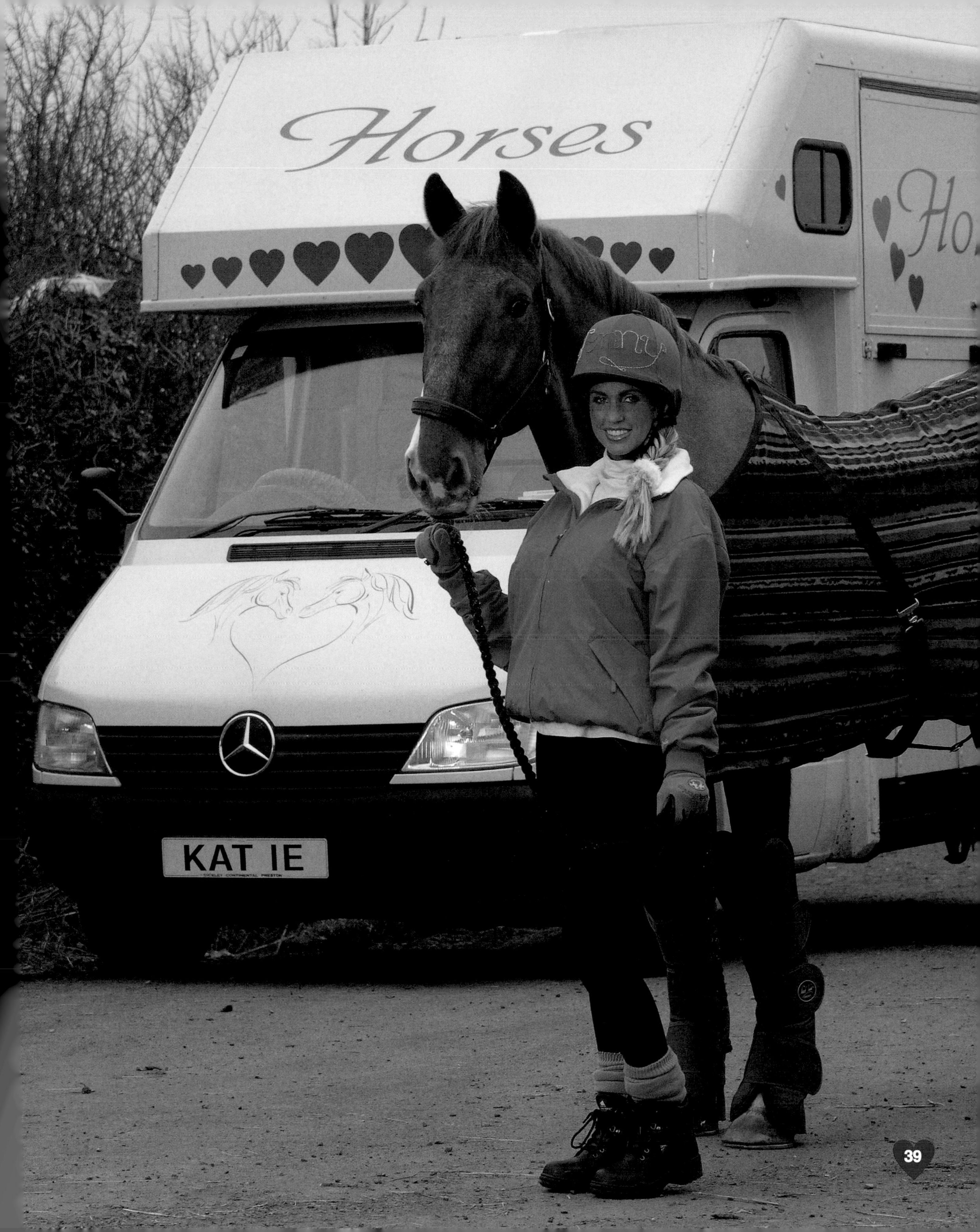
Horses
KAT IE

Your pony's home *Living outdoors*

Ponies love being out in the field with their mates. But you do need to look after them properly.

A pony living outdoors needs:

- **YOU** to come and see him every single day without fail, whatever the weather!

- **MATES** Ponies don't like to live alone and will want friends.

- **FOOD** Grass alone won't be enough in the winter when it's cold.

- **WATER** that is clean and fresh and that he can get to.

- **SHELTER** from the sun in the summer, and somewhere he and his pals can get out of the wind in the winter.

- **GOOD FENCES** Ponies can be expert at escaping! Barbed-wire fences are really dangerous. If this is what your field has, try and get everyone to club together for electric fencing. But remember that electric fencing is not enough on its own. Use it as a back-up for other fencing.

- **A WARM RUG** for nasty weather if he has a thin coat or is clipped.

- **LOTS OF HUGS AND KISSES!**

Danger, Danger!
Fields can harbour nasty plants that could be very dangerous for your pony. Ask someone knowledgeable to check your field for you. Look out, for instance, for yew, ragwort or acorns.

Looking after your outdoor pony

Brrr! – cold, wet winter days

In the winter, your pony will look forward to seeing you every day. He will probably be waiting at the gate for you. And he will definitely want to scoff down at least one good feed as well as having lots of hay to share with his mates.

How to feed hay in a field

- **DON'T** feed hay close to a gate or fence.

- **DO** put out at least one more pile of hay than there are ponies. If there are four ponies in the field, make sure you make at least five piles – ponies like to push each other around and the weakest pony could end up hungry.

- **DON'T** feed hay where the ground is badly 'poached' – trampled and muddy.

- **DO** check your pony's water trough every morning if it is very cold as the water might have frozen. If it has, you will have to break the ice! Take out all the chunks of ice, leaving just one bit to keep the water moving.

What is mud fever?

If a pony is always standing in wet, muddy conditions, the skin in his heels can get very sore and an infection can start. Lots of small scabs and sores will appear. This is called **mud fever**. You can protect against this by coating his heels in a protective oil (I use liquid paraffin or petroleum jelly) to stop the wet getting through. Also, don't trim your pony's feathers (the long hairs on the back of the fetlocks) in the winter, as they act like a water chute for rain running down his legs.

Sun, sun, sun – it's summertime

Ponies can pig out far too much when the grass is lush. If your pony looks like he's getting too fat, watch out for **laminitis**. This is an inflammation of the sensitive tissues in a pony's foot and is very dangerous. Make sure you know what to look out for – ask your vet or stable manager to help you recognize the danger signs.

Flies and midges can be a real pest for ponies in the summer. Make sure you put fly repellent on your pony every day. Use special wipes for around his eyes.

You can use a fly fringe or mask to keep flies out of your pony's eyes and ears. Make sure it's the sort that will break if he gets caught up on anything in the field.

Nasty but necessary. Pick out the poo from your pony's field in the summer or it will attract even more flies.

Don't let your pony get sunburn on his nose! You put on sunblock to protect yourself from the sun – do the same for your pony if he has a sensitive nose!

Your pony's mates

Ponies are herd animals. They love to be part of a big, mischievous gang and don't like to live on their own. When a pony has a very special friend, you might see them mutual grooming – grooming each other with their teeth. Imagine doing that to *your* best friend!

Your pony's home
Living indoors

If you decide to keep your pony in a stable, you will have to work extra-hard to make sure he has everything he needs.

Your stabled pony will need:

- **YOU** to come and see him every morning *and* every evening.

- **FOOD** Hay must be available. And he may need a feed in a bucket once or twice a day.

- **WATER** Two buckets of fresh water in his stable every night (two, in case he knocks one over).

- **A RUG** for the night in cold weather.

- **FRESH AIR** Make sure his stable has plenty of air and isn't dusty or stuffy.

- **SPACE** A typical pony loose box is probably a square about 3 metres wide. Make sure your pony has enough room to lie down and roll.

- **BEDDING** so he can lie down in his stable without hurting himself.

- **LOTS OF HUGS AND KISSES!**

Hay

A stabled pony will need hay.

- Weigh your hay so you know exactly how much you are feeding.

- Feed the best hay you can find. Cheap hay can be dusty or mouldy and could make your pony sick.

- If you use a hay-net make sure it is tied at the right height for your pony. Always tie it up using a quick- release knot.

Types of bedding

STRAW is my favourite. I love to see my horses lying down in nice, deep straw beds. They always have straw in their manes in the mornings!

WOOD SHAVINGS are very popular, and good for ponies with any breathing problems. They are easy to muck out too.

RUBBER MATTING drains well and is good as a base underneath other bedding.

Mucking out

A stable needs to be mucked out every single day. You don't want your pony to live in a dirty, smelly stable. Take out all the droppings and wet bedding before putting a fresh bed down for him. Your pony will love coming in to a clean stable with lots of nice bedding.

A nameplate for your pony's stable

Show everyone how much you love your pony by making him a special nameplate!

- Paint a piece of wood or bark your favourite colour, then paint on your pony's name. Use as many colours as you like to make this really funky.

- Keep one of his horseshoes, paint it with silver paint and nail this on the sign too.

- Get an adult to help you cut a nameplate in the shape of a horseshoe or a heart, then paint on your pony's name!

- Get your paints out and paint a picture of your pony on the sign.

- Glue your fave photo to the sign and paint it over with varnish to protect it.

Do ask your parent or other responsible adult to help you do this.

48

Important!

Don't put your pony's nameplate anywhere he can reach it or you might find he has spoiled all your hard work by nibbling at it!

Feeding your pony

Lots of ponies don't need more than grass in the summer, but will need feeding in the winter. Others, like a stabled pony, or a pony who is doing lots of work, will need more food. Make sure you know what you need to feed your pony. If in doubt, *ask someone experienced* to help you.

- **DO** let your pony have grass or hay available for most of the day. This is what a horse naturally eats.

- **DO** feed good quality feed.

- **DO** weigh your feed.

- **DON'T** make sudden changes.

- **DON'T** ride your pony within an hour of a bowl of feed. You wouldn't want to run around right after a big dinner, would you?

- **DO** make sure your pony always has water available.

- **NEVER** underfeed your pony because you think he would be easier to ride if he didn't have so much energy.

- **DON'T** *over*feed your pony either.

What to feed
Roughage
This is the bulk of your pony's diet. Grass is the most natural feed, often called 'Doctor Green' as it is so good for horses and ponies. When there is no grass available, feed hay or haylage instead. Chaff – which is chopped straw – also makes a base for other feeds in a dinner bucket.

Concentrates
If you want your pony to work hard for you, these are the feedstuffs that will give him 'oomph'. You can buy them ready-mixed like special pony nuts, or mixes. The bags give you advice on how much to feed, and they contain lots of useful vitamins and minerals, too, to help keep your pony super-healthy.

Special Treats

Ponies love treats – like peppermints and cut-up pieces of apple or carrot. Cut apples in quarters and carrots in long fingers – a greedy pony could try and gobble down a whole carrot and choke on it!

Save treats for special moments. Ponies can be very nippy if you always give them something to eat. A pat and a 'Good boy' or 'Good girl' is usually just as nice for them. Never go into a field and begin handing out treats. Ponies are smart. They will soon work out what's going on and come running and you could be knocked flying as they all try to get to you at once.

Pony-mad at home

You can still have lots of pony fun when you aren't with your pony.

My pony notebook
Keep details of everything you do with ponies. Or cut out your
favourite articles from magazines and keep them in a file.
Go pony-mad with the covers!

My pony noticeboard
Make sure you have all your favourite photos of your pony friends where you can see them every day.
Pin them up on a board, along with your rosettes, drawings of your pony and all your other pony things.

My pony mementos

You'll never forget your first rosettes, so make sure you have somewhere safe to keep them. And you might want to keep little bits of mane and tail from your favourite ponies to remind you what fun you had together. For all your pony keepsakes, turn a simple shoebox into a fab place to keep all these precious bits and pieces.

Cover the box in crepe paper, ask an adult to help you cut out silver-foil horseshoe shapes and stick them all over it, then add glitter . . .

Or try and make your box look like a pony manege. Mark in the letters of the schooling area to help you remember what 'Trot at A' means!

Your pony's health

I feel so, so sorry for any pony who is injured or sick. Sometimes it's just bad luck, but there are also things you **MUST** do to keep your pony healthy.

Vaccinations

Make sure your pony has his annual vaccinations so he doesn't get ill. And don't forget to give your pony a special big hug for being so good after he has had his jabs !

Teeth

Can you imagine someone putting a big file into your mouth and rasping your teeth? It sounds awful but your pony will probably enjoy it, especially if his teeth have been growing unevenly or rubbing sore spots in his mouth. Your vet can check his teeth, or there are special horse dentists.

Worming

Ponies that graze together should be wormed together. It's natural for your pony to pick up some worms – they pick up worm eggs from the grass. Special worming granules or pastes will kill the worms before they can grow big enough to harm your pony. Ask your vet about how often to worm.

Temperature

A pony's normal temperature is about 100 to 101.5 degrees F (38°C). To take his temperature, you have to push a thermometer into his bum and hold it there, so it's a good idea to ask someone experienced to do this for you.

Pulse rate

A pony's pulse rate shows how fast his heart beats each minute. Put two fingers under his chin by the jawbone and you can feel the beat. It should be between 36 and 42 beats.
Tip: if he's just been running around, it will be much higher. Wait until he's cooled down before counting again or you'll worry yourself for no reason.

Breathing rate

Look at your pony's belly and count it going in and out as he breathes. A normal pony will take about 8–12 breaths a minute.

Calling the vet

If in doubt, always call the vet out! Some illnesses – like colic (a blockage in his tummy or intestines) – can be really serious.

KATIE'S TIP

The best person to spot if your pony is feeling sick is the person who sees him every day and knows what is normal for him – this means YOU! If you think your pony isn't well and you don't know what to do, ask someone else or call the vet. Better to be safe than sorry.

If your pony is ill

he will need lots and lots of attention and care. Try to stick to your normal routine as much as possible, but give him extra big kisses too.

Your pony's shoes

Ponies' hooves keep on growing all the time, like your fingernails. This means they will need their hooves trimmed, or shoes fitted, about every six weeks.

Why shoe?

Most native ponies have hard feet and will only need their hooves trimmed. But if you ride a lot on hard surfaces – like on the road – your pony might need horseshoes fitted to protect his feet.

No foot, no horse!

It's an old saying, but it's often true! If a pony's feet are in trouble, you won't be able to ride him at all and he probably won't even be able to go out in the field with his mates until he is better. So it's very important to look after your pony's feet. Always check them and pick out any mud or stones every time you see him.

Handmade to fit!

The farrier fits the shoe to the foot. This means he heats the shoe and shapes it while it is hot to fit your pony. Don't worry – it won't hurt your pony. He can't feel the heat from the shoe.

Coronary band – this is where new hoof grows from. If your pony injures this area, his hoof might not grow down properly.

Trimming the hoof

Shaping the shoe

Nailing the shoe on

Frog – this is like a shock absorber for your pony. The frog cushions the impact of his feet on the ground.

KATIE'S TIP

If your pony hasn't had shoes fitted before, make sure he can lift and hold up each of his feet properly for the farrier. Farriers like well-behaved ponies.

57

Fun things to do with your pony

Riding lessons

Ponies love to get out and about and have fun with their riders. But to make sure you have the best possible time, it is important to learn to ride properly. Do what I did and go to your local riding school and have lessons before you think about owning your own pony. It will give you the chance to ride lots of different sorts of ponies, and you'll spend all week looking forward to your next riding lesson.

Learn how to:

- mount and dismount properly.
- walk, trot and canter.
- control your pony's speed and direction.
- apply the brakes! It's really handy to know this before you go out and gallop down a field. I used to get bombed off with all the time when I was first learning.

A pony's paces

Walking There are four beats to a walk stride. Back left, front left, back right, front right. Everyone begins with a walk. I remember thinking how far down it was to the ground! Now I ride a horse who is over 18 hands high…

Trotting This is two-time. Your pony springs alternately from one diagonal to another. When you trot in a circle and rise up and down with the rhythm, you should always sit down when the outside front leg is on the ground.

Canter This is three-time. For a left-lead canter (when you ride round with your left shoulder to the inside of the school, anti-clockwise), your pony will strike off with his back right leg first, then he will put the diagonal of back left and front right down at the same time for the second beat, and finally the front left leg last. For a right-lead canter, it's the other way round.

Left-lead canter

Beaches, barbecues, woods and lanes. . .

Riding out – hacking out – is so fantastic! I love to ride round fields and lanes on one of my horses. It's great to have fun in the country with your pony. If you go on a pony-mad holiday, you might be lucky enough to ride on a beach. Or high up the hills and along the banks of rivers.

In the summer

If flies bother your pony, fit a fly-mask

Hacking

In traffic

Always wear fluorescent safety gear if you and your pony go on the roads

In the woods

Treasure trails

Get together with your mates and set up a treasure trail.

1. Think up a prize in advance. Getting the losers to each muck out the winner's pony once is a popular prize. Everyone wants to win that!

2. Make up clues leading to places where you ride.

3. Tie a bunch of rosettes on each site, using a different colour for each. You can fix them to your bridles so the winner gets to ride in first on a fabulous colourful pony.

4. Sort everyone into pairs (it's more fun and safer, too).

5. Write down the clues on a piece of paper and give this to each pair. Now see who can solve them all quickest and get back to the yard first.

Fun clues

Use your imagination to make up the clues – you know your own yard. You could put the rosettes.

- where Molly bit Stormy last week on Sunday's hack.

- on the spooky drop fence that Killarney refuses to jump - ever!

- by the stream where Polo rolled just after he'd had a bath.

Add an extra challenge by testing everyone's pony know-how at the same time. For each colour rosette collected, make up a quiz question. Then you can give an extra prize to the rider with the most right answers.

Katie's quiz questions

Hint: you can find the answers in this book

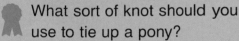

What sort of knot should you use to tie up a pony?

What should you always put on before getting on a pony?

Danger! Can you name two plants that are poisonous to ponies?

What is 'Doctor Green'?

What's a frog? (Not the green, croaky sort!)

What do you call a young boy horse up to the age of three?

What sort of ponies are measured in inches rather than hands?

Answers
pink: quick-release knot **blue:**
your hat **red:** yew and ragwort
green: grass **purple:** the soft,
squashy, shock absorber bit in the
middle of a pony's sole **red and**
white: a colt **blue and gold:**
Shetland ponies – like my Rosie!

Fancy dress competitions

I always love dressing up and it's great fun to dress up yourself and your pony for a fancy-dress competition. Go wild – think up something special, ask your parent or a responsible adult to help you make your costume and surprise everyone!

KATIE'S TIP

Make sure your pony sees your costume and is happy with it before you try and get in the saddle. And don't dress him up with anything that might frighten him.

Woooo.....!

Ghosties and ghoulies and things that go bump in the night...

Lucky black cat.

Putting a spell on you!

Other costumes could include a ghost (use a big white sheet!) or a little imp. And as apples are traditional for Halloween, you and your mates can go apple bobbing and let your ponies eat the apples afterwards!

Ho, ho, ho! Merry Christmas to all the ponies you love.

The angel from the top of the tree

Santa's elf helper

KATIE'S TIP

If it's cold at Christmas, don't let your pony get a chill. Feel the base of his ears to see if he is warm enough. If they feel cold you should put a rug over him before you show off your costume.

Santa on his reindeer

Fun in the sun for a summer show extravaganza

Pocahontas

Here comes the bride

Pretty princess

Use leg bandages to decorate your pony's legs. Make sure they are fitted properly.

A play on horseback

Summer is the perfect time to get together with your mates and put on a play on horseback. You could perform this to help raise money for your local pony rescue centre maybe, or for a special birthday party. Why not try a story about fairies rescuing a poor little unicorn?

Mounted games

Ponies love playing games as much as you do and it's a great way to develop your riding skills too. Here are some of my favourites.

Ball and bucket
How many balls can your team get in the bucket?!

Bending poles
In and out of the poles and back to the start again! It's a real test of your riding skill as you have to keep changing direction. If you don't have any poles, use upturned buckets, or a row of big carrots to mark the places.

Relay races
Teams of three riders who must pass the baton to each other. What's fun is if the first rider has to do their leg at a walk, the second at a trot, and the third at a fast canter!

Musical statues
Excited ponies hate to stand still, so this is a fab way of practising making your pony halt well. Everyone rides round to music. Each time the music stops, you have to halt and then the person with the music shouts out 'Freeze!' and everyone has stay completely still. The first pony to move is o-u-t!

Water pistols
This is really messy. Each team has a water pistol and a bucket to squirt water in. One at a time, you have to fill your pistol, ride up to the bucket and squirt it in, then race back to the start. The team that gets the most water into their bucket within a set time wins.

Why not make up your own games? Make sure they are safe for your pony and then practise and practise and you can challenge all your mates, or another pony club.

Dance with your pony

When riding, music can help you keep a nice rhythm e.g. when trotting, pick a song with a two-time beat.

In recent years, dressage to music has become really popular – I call it dancing with a horse or pony, because that's what you are doing. Walking, trotting, cantering – all in time to music you have chosen. Try it!

Isn't this pony beautiful!

Katie's playlist

Here are some of my favourites to ride to. Ask a parent or other responsible adult to help you record bits of the music one after the other on a tape, so you can change the pace several times.

Walk

This needs a slow four-time beat. My husband Pete's Top Ten hit, *Mysterious Girl*, is perfect for this. Or you could try an old favourite like *My Four-Legged Friend*.

Trot

This is a two-time beat so there are lots of pop and dance songs that would be perfect. One of my favourites is the bouncy song from *Mary Poppins*: *Supercalifragilisticexpialidocious*.

Canter

You can't beat one of the really pretty ballet songs like the *Sleeping Beauty Waltz* – it's a tune that always makes me feel like a princess.

KATIE'S TIP

If dancing as a group, make sure everyone knows where they are supposed to be going. Always pass left shoulder to left shoulder if going at the same pace.

Shows

I love to take my horses to shows and let everyone see how clever and smart they are. It's also fun to compete. When I began riding, I used to take my scruffy pony along to shows where there were lots of girls with really posh ponies, but me and Star still had lots of fun together – and we learned a lot too.

Here's me and Tyke now, all dressed up and ready for a show. Doesn't Tyke look magnificent!

Going to shows with your pony

Go on, have a go! It's lots of fun and you'll never forget winning your first rosette.

Best turned out pony and rider

This is a class that everyone can enter. It's a competition to see who has groomed their pony best, and looks smartest themselves. You have to be spotless! Your pony has to be shining and your tack gleaming. Even a bit of mud on your own boots will lose you points, but everyone can have fun polishing up themselves and their pony and having a go at this class.

Fun classes

Don't despair if you haven't got the smartest pony or all the right gear. There are lots of fun classes you can enter too.

- Pony with the longest mane

- Pony the judge most wants to take home

- The most handsome gelding

- The prettiest mare

- Best veteran in hand (great for the oldest ponies)

KATIE'S TIP

To practise going to shows you could run your own show at your stables or with your pony club. Ask someone experienced to help you organize it.

Handy pony

When you ride one special pony all the time, you can build a lovely relationship between the two of you. You know he is clever and smart. You trust him, and he trusts you. Handy pony competitions are fantastic for showing everyone else what a perfect pair you are. They test pony and rider in a series of everyday challenges.

KATIE'S TIP

Learn how to ride your pony past scary objects. You'll need to know how to turn his head away from the object. but still use your legs to keep him moving forward in a good straight line. Ask your riding teacher if you can practise this in lessons.

A typical course could include:

- riding in and out of bending poles.

- opening a small gate without dismounting – this tests how well you can control your pony.

- riding past scary road bollards – does your pony trust you enough?

- making your pony halt and stand still for a certain length of time – ponies can be so fidgety!

- stepping over a row of poles laid out on the ground.

- dismounting, leading your pony properly and then remounting.

- a low jump – like a small tree trunk.

- taking off your pony's saddle and leading him to the finish line.

- riding past a bunch of bright balloons.

Jumping

Jumping my horses is one of my favourite things. It's a fantastic feeling, soaring through the air on the back of a horse. All horses and ponies jump naturally. But it's very important to do it properly.

- **DON'T** ever jump without wearing a back protector.

- **DO** take lessons first.

- **DON'T** ever jump on your own.

- **DON'T** think your pony is a jumping machine. If you jump your pony too much, he will get fed up.

- **DON'T** try and jump a big jump just cos your mates can. Their ponies might be more experienced.

- **DO** warm your pony up first. Never just tack him up and go straight out to jump.

- **DO** fit protective boots to your pony's legs if appropriate.

- **DO** reward your pony when he's tried his best.

- **DO** have fun and make sure your pony does too.

KATIE'S TIP

Always learn the course well before you go out to jump. If you get lost, or miss out a jump, you will be eliminated. Don't practise loads with your pony before the show, and then get knocked out just because you forgot where to go.

Showjumping

Jumps – like brightly coloured poles, imitation bricks built into walls, and white gates – are built in an arena and have to be jumped in a particular order.

Faults
Faults are given for refusals (3 faults for a refusal, and you're out if you have 3 refusals on the course) and knockdowns (4 faults). There may also be time faults if you take too long over the whole course.

Clear round jumping
Every rider who jumps clear – nothing knocked down, and no refusals – wins a rosette. This is great fun, and you will be so proud of your pony!

Walking the course
Most riders like to walk round a course before trying to jump it. You can work out which jumps you think might be tricky for you and your pony.

Jump-offs
In some classes, if lots of riders go clear, there may be a jump-off. Ponies jump again, this time against the clock. Really nippy ponies love these classes.

Pony and Pooch
Now your dog can join in the fun too. First you jump the course on your pony, then you have to dismount and jump it again – with your dog. Add up the combined faults to find the winner!

Cross-country jumping

Jumping outdoor obstacles is a real challenge to you and your pony and you should only try this once you are an experienced rider.

You could have to jump:
ditches, banks, step ups and **step downs** (like a sunken road), **logs** or **tree trunks, barrels, gates, water, hay bales**, jumps made out of **brush or twisted branches, car** or **lorry tyres, post** and **rail fences** or other natural obstacles.

Sponsored cross-country days
Raise money for charity and have fun at the same time. Sponsored rides are rides of around 4 to 8 miles, with 10 to 20 jumps which are easy enough for everyday riders. Your family and friends sponsor you for each jump. You don't have to jump anything if you don't want to, so you can miss out any which you find too scary, or which are too big for your pony.

KATIE'S TIP

Watch out for for jumps that look easy to you but are designed to be scary to your pony. A good example is a low log jump into dark woods. The jump looks easy, but the woods make it super-scary for your pony.

Goodnight to your pony

If you come home from a show, no matter how tired you feel, make sure you take care of your pony first.

A big yawn for this pony!

If he lives outdoors . . .

- brush him down
- feed and rug as normal for the time of year
- then take him out to the field to see his mates
- watch him trot off happily and have a roll!

If he lives indoors . . .

- brush him down
- feed and rug as normal for the time of year
- make sure he has a nice, deep bed for the night and enough hay
- lead him into his stable
- watch him tuck into his hay and have a good roll in his bedding

And this one . . .

And don't forget to give your pony **A BIG GOODNIGHT HUG**

and **A BIG GOODNIGHT KISS** for being so special . . .

83

Goodnight, pony!

Katie Price and Random House Children's Books would like to thank the following
for their help in the preparation of this book:

Derby House for providing equestrian clothing for Katie Price for the book
(except where items were model's own); for clothing for the young riders (except where items
are models' own), for horse rugs on pages 36, 37 and 38, and for the ponies' headcollars.
www.derbyhouse.co.uk

Jodie Maile, BHS AI, Int. Stable Manager, for a qualified check on the content of the book.

Photography sessions carried out at:
Snowball Farm Equestrian Centre, Buckinghamshire
With thanks to Charles Western-Kaye and staff, and ponies Angel, Blackie, Holly,
Molly, Phoenix, Robin, Salam, Splash, Straggy, Tanya and Toffee.
www.snowballfarm.co.uk

and at:
Plumpton Agricultural College, Equine Department, Sussex
www.plumpton.ac.uk

With thanks to the staff, horses Jelly and Tyke, and ponies Nemo, Midnight, Princess and Tasie.

Thanks also to our models: Beth, Elle, Emma, Diani, Grace, Suzi and Sophie.

Katie Price photography by Can Associates Limited
Styled by Kerrie-Ann Keogh
Hair and make-up by Gary Cockerill

Snowball Farm photography by Danny Elewes

Design by Mandy Sherliker
Editorial by Sue Cook and Lucy Walker
Props by Chris Fraser
Diagrams by Jo Buchan

Important notes to parents/guardians

If your child wants to own a pony, you need to know that this is a huge commitment. Ponies can live as long as 35 or 40 years and will need daily attention. Buying a pony is easy (and sometimes not very expensive) but looking after one properly is neither easy nor easily affordable.

- Make sure you have enough time, and enough money, to look after a pony properly.
- Talk to your child's riding school to find out more about the costs of looking after a pony, and what livery facilities are available in your area.
- Make sure you buy a pony that is suitable for your child and for his or her riding abilities. Their riding instructor should be able to help. If you are buying a pony they don't know, ask if they will go with you and help you see if it is suitable.
- Call the British Horse Society (or the equivalent in other countries) for free advice, leaflets and details of recommended riding schools and livery yards in your area.

Every pony needs:

- to be visited at least once a day, more likely twice, every day for what could be over twenty years, depending on the age of your pony.
- a place to live, which includes other ponies for company.
- feed, bedding, clothing and equipment.
- a visit from the farrier approximately every six weeks.
- worming regularly.
- vaccinations.
- any other veterinary treatment that might be required. Vet bills can be enormous if your pony has a bad accident and the pony won't be able to be ridden while ill or injured.
- insurance.

Are you prepared to spend lots of time standing around at stables while your child looks after his or her pony? To spend weekends at horse shows if your child wants to compete? To make difficult decisions when your child outgrows the pony and wants a bigger pony or a horse, but also wants to keep their special friend?

If I haven't put you off, that's GREAT! But do make sure you know what you are taking on first. Every pony deserves a good home.

Katie xxx

Picture Acknowledgements

Page 1
Rosette © Valerie Loiseleux; Horseshoe
© Christine Balderas: both supplied by iStockphoto.

Pages 2-3
Katie Price with Star © Syriol James/More, supplied
by Camerapress. Wedding carriage © Katie Price,
supplied by CAN Associates.

Pages 6-7
Girl with brush © David Walters of HORSEPIX.
Girl holding horse © Danny Elewes.

Pages 8-9
Two ponies © iStockphoto. Other pony images
© Eline Spek, supplied by iStockphoto.

Pages 10-11
Horse image © Ramon Berk, supplied by iStockphoto.

Pages 12-13
Shetland pony © Eline Spek; Single pony
© Rob Sylvan; Two ponies © Simon Phipps:
all supplied by iStockphoto.

Pages 14-15
From top: images © Robert Maxwell,
© Arjan de Jager; © Jeroen Peys; © Barry Crossley;
© Hendrik De Bruyne: all supplied by iStockphoto.

Pages 16-17
Pony's tail and foot in stirrup © Danny Elewes.
Shoes © Cloki, supplied by iStockphoto.
Girls in riding hats © Danny Elewes.

Pages 18-19
All girl and pony images © Danny Elewes.

Pages 20-21
Girl with pony; Grooming box: © Danny Elewes.

Pages 22-23
All girl and pony images © Danny Elewes.

Pages 24-25
Girl washing pony's tail © Danny Elewes.

Pages 26-27
All images © Danny Elewes.

Pages 28-29
Girl with pony; Pony in blue bridle: © Danny Elewes.
Pony in red bridle by Can Associates Limited.

Pages 30-31
All images © Danny Elewes.

Pages 32-33
Ponies in browbands © Danny Elewes.

Pages 34-35
All images © Danny Elewes.

Pages 36-37
All images © Danny Elewes.

Pages 38-39
Girl holding pony © Danny Elewes. Horse
looking out of horsebox © Angela Hill,
supplied by iStockphoto.

Pages 40-41
Grey pony grazing © iStockphoto; Palomino pony
in pasture © Melissa Jones; Pony in snow
© Mikhail Kondrashov: all supplied by iStockphoto.

Pages 42-43
Pony images © Danny Elewes.

Pages 44-45
Large image © iStockphoto; Top inset © Atlanpic;
Bottom inset © Barry Crossley: all supplied
by iStockphoto.

Pages 46-47
Pony; Girl with pony: © Danny Elewes.

Pages 50-51
Girl with hay © Alamy/ImageState.

Pages 54-55
Pony image by Can Associates Limited.

Pages 56-57
Trimming the hoof © Steven Robertson;
Shaping the shoe © Stacey Bates; Nailing the shoe
© Verity Johnson: all supplied by iStockphoto.
Pony's hoof by Can Associates Limited.

Pages 58-59
Girl in white t-shirt on pony © Tina Lorien, supplied
by iStockphoto. Girl in pink on pony © Danny Elewes.

Pages 60-61
Main image of ponies by sea © Clive Green;
Girl and pony in woods © Andrew Martin;
Two girls and ponies hacking © Barry Crossley:
all supplied by iStockphoto. Pony in fly-mask;
Girl in safety gear and pony: © Danny Elewes.

Pages 62-63
Girl leading horse © David Walters of HORSEPIX.
Girl on pony © Hedda Gjerpen, supplied
by iStockphoto.

Pages 64-65
Girls on ponies all © Danny Elewes. Pumpkin ©
Jim Jurica; Apple © Daniella Barioglio: supplied
by iStockphoto.

Pages 66-67
All images © Danny Elewes.

Pages 68-69
All images © Danny Elewes.

Pages 70-71
Girl in blue hat on pony © Verity Johnson;
Girl in brown jumper on pony © Hedda Gjerpen:
both supplied by iStockphoto. Girl in cream gloves
© Getty Images/Johner.

Pages 74-75
Girl in black hat on pony; Girl in pink hat on pony:
© Danny Elewes. Trophy © Christine Balderas;
Girl holding pony © Philip Downs;
Pony with mane © Stacey Bates: all supplied
by iStockphoto.

Pages 76-77
Girls on ponies © Danny Elewes. Balloons
© James Steidl, supplied by iStockphoto.

Pages 78-79
Girl on pony © Danny Elewes.

Pages 80-81
Dog image © Emmanuelle Bonzamai;
Girl jumping on chestnut © Hedda Gjerpen;
Girl jumping on piebald © John Rich;
Girl and water © Eline Spek: all supplied
by iStockphoto.

Pages 82-83
Grey pony yawning © iStockphoto;
Chestnut pony © Jorge Lopez Oviano:
supplied by iStockphoto.